TERRORIST TRAINING CAMPS IN IRAN

How Islamic Revolutionary Guards Corps
Trains Foreign Fighters to Export Terrorism

A Publication of National Council of Resistance of Iran
U.S. Representative Office

Terrorist Training Camps in Iran; How Islamic Revolutionary Guards Corps Trains Foreign Fighters to Export Terrorism

First published in 2017 by
National Council of Resistance of Iran—U.S. Representative Office (NCRI-US), 1747 Pennsylvania Ave., NW, Suite 1125, Washington, DC 20006

ISBN-10: 1-944942-06-8
ISBN-13: 978-1-944942-06-9

ISBN-10: 1-944942-07-6 (e-book)
ISBN-13: 978-1-944942-07-6 (e-book)

Library of Congress Control Number: 2017945390

Library of Congress Cataloging-in-Publication Data

National Council of Resistance of Iran—U.S. Representative Office.
Presidential Elections in Iran; Changing Faces; Status Quo Policies

Iran. 2. Terrorism. 3. Revolutionary Guards. 4. Middle East. 5. Syria

First Edition: June 2017

Printed in the United States of America

Table of Contents

1

INTRODUCTION

The following information has been gathered and documented by the social network of the People's Mojahedin Organization of Iran (PMOI/MEK) inside Iran. The revelations are made public by the National Council of Resistance of Iran—US Representative Office (NCRI-US).

Article 151 of the Iranian regime's Constitution specifies the duties of the Islamic Revolutionary Guards Corp (or IRGC) as "protecting the Revolution and its accomplishments." To put it another way, the IRGC is the backbone of the apparatus established to preserve the dictatorship, which itself rests on three pillars: the first is suppression within Iran; the second is export of terrorism and fundamentalism beyond Iran's borders; and the third is the program to manufacture a nuclear bomb and nuclear-capable missiles to threaten other countries.

The Revolutionary Guards is involved in military and terrorist interference in several countries of the region. Within the borders of Iran's neighbors, extensive terrorist operations and military meddling are carried out simultaneously. The IRGC also organizes terrorist networks and conducts terrorist operations throughout the world.

According to detailed reports from inside the clerical regime, the Islamic Revolutionary Guard Corps (IRGC) has created a large directorate within its extraterritorial arm, the Quds Force, in order to expand its training of foreign mercenaries as part of the strategy to step up its meddling abroad in Syria, Iraq, Yemen, Bahrain, Afghanistan and elsewhere. The overhaul has occurred with the blessing of Supreme Leader Ali Khamenei, who according to a senior adviser to the IRGC commander-in-chief and the directorate's former commander, IRGC Brigadier General Khosrow Orouj, personally applauded its creation during a recent visit to the Quds Force.

The intelligence reports, gathered over several months by various sources of the MEK's network from inside different units of the IRGC, especially the Quds Force, indicate that this directorate has dozens of training camps across Iran. The camps have been assigned based on the nationality of the trainees and the type of training. Both terrorist training and military training for militias are provided, enabling them to better infiltrate and advance the regime's regional objectives.

Every month, hundreds of forces from Iraq, Syria, Yemen, Afghanistan and Lebanon—countries where the regime is involved in frontline combat—receive military training and are subsequently dispatched to wage terrorism and war. Smaller groups are also trained in other countries in order to conduct terrorist acts and operations. Since 2012, there has been an increase in the extent of training of foreign mercenaries in IRGC-controlled camps of the Quds Force.

For operations in countries where there is no open warfare—including Persian Gulf countries such as Bahrain and Kuwait—terrorists cells are trained instead.

2

THE QUDS FORCE TRAINING DIRECTORATE

The Quds Force Training Directorate (group) forms an important part of the terrorist Quds Force. In internal IRGC communications, the codename of the Quds Force Training Directorate is 12,000. The headquarters is located at the Imam Ali military base, at kilometer 20 of the Tehran-Karaj highway, Ardestani Boulevard, close to the end of Saravan Street. The site is comprised of a large complex housing several IRGC garrisons; the Imam Ali Garrison is situated in the southeastern quadrant. The area of the

Qods Force Commander IRGC General Qassem Soleimani

Imam Ali Garrison alone is about 10 hectares (350m x 330m), about 25 acres. The logistics section of the Imam Ali Garrison is located in another part of this complex, the so-called Mostafa Khomeini Garrison, which has a separate entrance and exit.

The Iranian resistance has so far identified 15 training centers belonging to the directorate.

Organization and Command

The commander of the Quds Training Directorate is a veteran Quds commander who reports directly to Quds Commander Qassem Soleimani. The group's commander for several years until 2015 was Brigadier General Rahimi. Before Rahimi, IRGC Brigadier General Khosrow Orouj held the position. Previously, Orouj was the IRGC commander in Lebanon, where he had a close relationship with the Lebanese Hezbollah. He participated in the 33-day war in Lebanon and was a friend of Imad Mughniyeh, a senior member of Islamic Jihad and Hezbollah.

IRGC Brigadier General Khosrow Orouj

In an interview in November 2016, Orouj said: "I was in charge of training for the Quds Force, and later took charge of training of the Quds Special Forces, working with them round-the-clock, going back and forth to Lebanon. ... When Khamenei visited the Quds Force, the only unit that he applauded was that same training unit." His remarks underscore Khamenei's close relationship with this terrorist training initiative, as well as Khamenei's reliance on the IRGC to advance the regime's agenda and objectives.

Brigadier General Seyyed Shafi Shafiee had been Deputy Commander of the training directorate starting from 2014. Prior to that, he was stationed in Syria. He was transferred back to Syria in 2016, where he was killed in combat in the Khan Tuman area in the vicinity of Aleppo in May 2016.

Brigadier General Seyyed Shafi Shafiee killed near Aleppo in May 2016

A senior Quds Force commander runs the training directorate, meaning that he is exclusively assigned to managing its affairs.

The Inspection commander is Massih Mohammadi. The Intelligence Protection commander is IRGC Colonel Bakhtiari.

3
TRAINING PROCESS

Imam Ali Garrison

In addition to housing the headquarters of the training directorate, the Imam Ali Garrison is one of its main training centers. There are two types of training: Basic training is short-term, usually only about 45 days, because the objective of this regimen, especially for Syrian mercenaries, is to use them in military actions similar to those of the IRGC Bassij force.

There is also full military training with specialized courses for those who are hired by the Quds Force on a permanent basis. Terrorist training courses are given as well. These take about nine and sometimes up to twelve months to complete.

Terrorist training

In addition to the forces who are trained for military action as part of the regime's overall meddling in the region, terrorist units of the Quds Force are also trained in separate, secret units for dispatch to various countries in the Persian Gulf area, Asia, Africa, and Latin America. Individuals who are trained for terrorist operations are kept separately and in isolation. They have a detached suite inside Imam Ali Garrison with a capacity of between 10 to 100 people. In most cases, terrorist training is given to teams of two people who are not in contact with other units of two.

In recent years, the IRGC has brought back a number of its agents from Latin America, including Venezuela, Uruguay, Paraguay and Bolivia, to the Imam Ali Garrison for training, leaving them in the hands of the Quds Force. These people were held in isolation and their presence and identities were kept top secret. The commander in charge of training for these forces is Colonel Tahmasebi.

All forces to undergo trained, initially go through a body-building boot camp for one week. The body-building group's commander is an IRGC commander named Mowlaee. Subsequently, specialized training is given in other training centers of the Quds Force. Upon completion of this period, all forces return once again to the Imam Ali Garrison, where a final exam and confirmation process is administered. In effect, the final recruiting is performed at this garrison.

Different sections of the training directorate in Imam Ali Garrison

1. Specialized training for heavy weaponry: The commander of this section, which is identified by codename 320, is Colonel Ali Mohammad. It has 3 sub-sections: drones, rockets, heavy weapons and heavy weapons maintenance.

2. Missile training: This course has two sections, theoretical and practical. The theoretical training portion is carried out with the help of simulators. After completion of the primary course, forces go to Semnan base to receive practical training in firing missiles.

3. Marine training.

4. Paratrooper training.

5. VIP security training (also known as "Protocol"): The commander of this section is Colonel Ramky, who is from Amol in northern Iran.

Composition of Trainee Units

In recent years, the largest contingent trained in Imam Ali Garrison came from Syria, at some points involving up to 230 trainees per session. In addition, the Quds Iraqi forces (Shia militias) go to this garrison to receive missile training. Mercenaries from other countries, such as Yemen, Lebanon and Bahrain, also receive training at this base.

Subsequent to the increased meddling of the Iranian regime in Syria, the number of training courses in Imam Ali Garrison has increased. Some of the mullahs from Qom's Al-Mustafa Community were also trained in the garrison and subsequently sent to Syria. A large number of people from Bahrain also took training courses here.

In addition to Imam Ali Garrison, the Iranian resistance has identified the following training centers belonging to the IRGC:

Imam Ali Academy in Tajrish, Tehran

Theoretical Training

IRGC mercenaries are first sent to this center for theoretical courses promoting fundamentalism and terrorism, and subsequently sent to other centers for practical training. This site was previously the headquarters of the Quds Force Training Directorate and used for practical terrorist training. However, after it was exposed, it was divided into two parts, one of which was transferred to the Imam Ali Garrison (mentioned above) and the other to Baadindeh Center in Varamin (mentioned below). The address for Imam Ali Academy is: Alborz Street in Tajrish, Saad Abad district in Northern Tehran, North of Saad Abad Palace.

Baadindeh Center in Varamin

Urban Training

Urban warfare and guerilla training, including riding motorcycles for terrorist operations, is provided at this center. Driving courses and various vehicle maneuvering courses are also provided. One of these exercises is related to freeing hostages, and is carried out inside buildings designated for training purposes The commander of this center is an IRGC commander named Ebrahimi. The center is located 30 km south of Varamin in the Siah Kouh region. The location is considered to be in a protected IRGC area in the vicinity of a number of secret IRGC sites. A portion of the Quds Training Directorate was transferred to this area after relocation from the Imam Ali Academy (in northern Tajrish). The site is codenamed 950.

Malek Ashtar Camp in Amol

Survival Training

One of the Quds Force training centers is situated in Oscou Mahalleh in Amol on the way towards Imamzadeh Hashem, in Mazandaran Province. Here, trainees undergo courses on how to survive under harsh conditions in the wilderness.

Semnan Center

Practical Missile Training

Training on firing missiles, including Katyusha rockets, Falagh missiles, and others, is provided at this center to Quds Force agents who first complete theoretical training sessions using simulators at Imam Ali Garrison. For instance, a number of Iraqi forces went to this base in 2014 to learn how to use various types of missiles, including Katyushas. Semnan is the regime's main missile center, and is the location of the recent IRGC missile tests. This week, it also paraded its missiles at the site.

Mashhad Center

Focus on Training Afghan Forces

At this training center in Mashhad (northeastern Iran), identified by the code 4000, forces mostly made up of Afghans are trained in groups of 300. This center has contacts with the Ansar Corps of the Quds Force, which is responsible for eastern Iran and Afghanistan.

Pazouki Garrison

Focus on Afghan Forces to be Dispatched to Syria

This Quds Force garrison is located in Varamin (southeastern Tehran) near Jalilabad village. In each training session, 200 Afghans are trained for deployment to Syria. Infantry training includes Kalashnikovs, machine guns, mortars, tactics, and sniper, among others. All instructors are from the Iranian Revolutionary Guard Corps (IRGC) and the Quds Force. After completion of the military training, trainees are assigned to the Fatimiyoun division. Each week, 200 to 300 fighters are sent to Syria. The garrison is located beside the IRGC Jalilabad base, and is a spin-off. Seyyed Mostafa Hosseini, a Quds Force commander, commands the Pazouki Garrison.

Lowshan Garrison

Special Training

This garrison is located near the city of Manjil bordering the city of Lowshan. The IRGC operates a large training base in this region called the Imam Khomeini base. A portion of the base has been provided to the Quds Force.

Chamran Garrison

Focus on Afghan Forces for Dispatch to Syria

This garrison is located 5 km from Jalilabad Garrison in the town of Pishwa in southeastern Tehran. At least 100 people take part in each training session, most of whom are Afghans residing in Iran, and are trained for deployment to Syria. The commander of the Chamran Garrison is Colonel Hosseini Moqaddam. Individuals receive sniper, mortar, and tactical training at this location.

Telecabin Axis

Commando Training

This center is an active training center of the Quds Force in northern Tehran. It has contacts with the location codenamed 950 (mentioned above), and specializes in providing commando training.

Abadan

Diving and Marine Training

At this location in southern Iran, diving and marine training is provided.

Ahwaz

Marine Training

Also in southern Iran, marine training is provided at this location

Qeshm Axis

Marine Training Courses

Also in southern Iran, Qeshm Axis provides marine training.

Shahriar Garrison

This garrison is one of the training centers of the Quds Force located in southwestern Tehran. It serves as the rendezvous point for Afghan mercenaries before their deployment to Syria from the cities of Qom, Tehran and Delijan. Currently, 2,000 Afghans are sent to Syria from this site every week. Each group stays for as long as two months in Syria, after which they are replaced by the next contingent. An officer of the Quds Force by the name of Khavari is in charge of sending troops to Syria from Shahriar Garrison.

More Training Sites Operated by the IRGC

The locations described above are a representative sample of only a portion of the IRGC sites provided to the Quds Force in conjunction with IRGC meddling activities outside Iran in recent years. The IRGC operates dozens of other, similar bases and camps, especially near the Iran-Iraq frontier, to enable it to interfere in Iraqi affairs. They have not been mentioned in this report.

It has been made clear in the course of investigations of these locations, that all of the centers and garrisons of the IRGC operated by the Quds Force are dedicated to this force for the training of mercenaries and foreign fighters. In addition to the Qods Force, other IRGC branches, including ground forces, marines, and missile units, also contribute to the regime's regional interference, committing their forces, resources and weapons to ensure that terrorist operations are carried out and the regime's plans to advance its agenda of warmongering and regional expansionism are realized. The scope of the IRGC's casualties during the wars in Syria and Iraq underscore this point.

4

QODS FORCE, AN INTEGRAL PART OF THE IRGC

The distinction between the Islamic Revolutionary Guards Corps (IRGC) and the Qods Force is unwarranted. It was fashioned by the Iranian regime to whitewash the atrocities perpetrated by the IRGC and its role in terrorism and intervention throughout the Middle East and beyond.

The Qods Force was formed in 1990. The Hezbollah in Lebanon, the Badr Brigade in Iraq and other terrorist entities affiliated with the Iranian regime were set up before the Qods Force was even established. The IRGC was directly responsible for the creation of these terrorist entities. Indeed, the Badr Brigade was originally an official military branch of the IRGC's ground forces and took part in different operations.

The Qods Force is part of the IRGC. Neither in the Iranian Constitution, nor in the budget, is there any reference to the Qods Force as a separate entity.

The Qods Force is a military entity consisting of IRGC units and divisions, as well as mercenary fighters the IRGC has trained. In other words, the Qods Force is not an independent and autonomous entity, nor does it have independent fighting forces. For example, fighters identified as Qods Force units in Syria are in reality part of a brigade from the IRGC's 19th Fajr Brigade, based in Shiraz. This brigade has been stationed in Syria for the past two years. Other Qods Force elements in Syria are mercenary forces from other countries.

Currently, the IRGC as a whole is involved in the wars in Syria and Iraq. The main fighting force is from the IRGC, and the casualties are essentially commanders of different IRGC ground force units, which makes it abundantly clear that the entirety of the IRGC as well as its forces in different provinces are involved in wars and terrorism in different countries. Similarly, the IRGC's navy and missile units are also involved. It is the IRGC which funds, trains and arms terrorist groups such as Hezbollah, Asa'eb Al Ahl-Haq and Kata'eb in Iraq.

In essence, the IRGC is the pillar that preserves the ruling religious dictatorship in Iran, by engaging in domestic repression, external terrorism and nuclear weapons and missile production.

As far as the domestic scene is concerned, the IRGC has four tasks:

1. The Ground Forces have been restructured into provincial forces to prevent the outbreak of popular uprisings.

2. It has set up the Khatam al-Anbia Garrison and its affiliated companies to control the nation's economy.

3. Through the IRGC's Intelligence Directorate, its Cyber Army and the Bassij, the IRGC controls social networks and arrests social media users.

4. Through its Counter-Intelligence Directorate, the IRGC controls the regime's officials and personnel, and even arrests them.

As for the nuclear weapons program, since 1984, the IRGC has sought to procure or manufacture nuclear weapons through the IRGC research center. This center later evolved into SPND, which is headed by Brig. Gen. Mohsen Fakhrizadeh. The IRGC is working to produce Shahab missiles, which are nuclear warhead capable. It has engaged in repeated tests to this end.

With regard to exporting terrorism and warmongering, the IRGC is involved in military and terrorist intervention in regional countries. It organizes terrorist networks and conducts terrorist operations throughout the world.

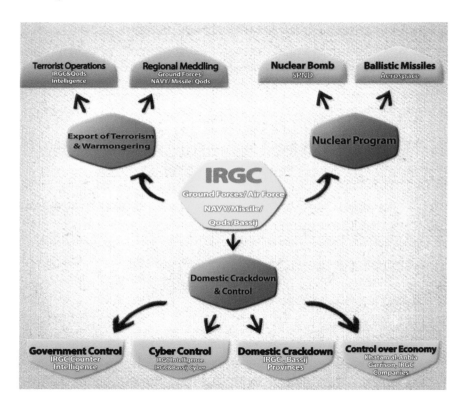

5

DOES THE IRGC MEET THE CRITERIA FOR DESIGNATION AS A FOREIGN TERRORIST ORGANIZATION?

The Islamic Revolutionary Guards Corps is not only engaged in the suppression of the people of Iran, but it has also been behind the nuclear weapons program of Iran and terrorism in the region and around the globe.

The IRGC continues, to date, to be engaged in terrorism and terrorist activities.

The Islamic Revolutionary Guards Corps (IRGC) meets the criteria to be designated as a Foreign Terrorist Organization (FTO), because it meets all of the three criteria as stated in the statute. It is:

1. A foreign entity.

2. Engages in terrorism, or terrorist activity or has the capability and intent to engage in terrorist activity.

3. Its terrorism threatens the national security of the United States or American nationals.

6

ESSENTIAL STEPS TO CONFRONT THE CRADLE OF ISLAMIC EXTREMISM

- It is high time that the Iranian regime be held accountable for its crimes against the people of Iran and the region, in particular for its killing of 120,000 Iranian dissidents, as well as its role as the world's leading state-sponsor of terrorism.

- The Islamic Revolutionary Guards Corps (IRGC) must be designated as a Foreign Terrorist Organization for engaging in terrorism and terrorist activities.

- The entire IRGC must be targeted with new sanctions, and any foreign entity that deals with it be subject to sanctions as well.

- Immediate measures must be taken to expel the IRGC from regional states, in particular Syria, Iraq and Yemen. This is the first step towards resolving the crises encompassing the region. At the same time that the United States is spending billions fighting ISIS in Iraq, the IRGC and its mercenaries are operating freely. This cycle can and must be ended.

APPENDICES

Location of 15 IRGC Terrorist Training Camps Around Iran

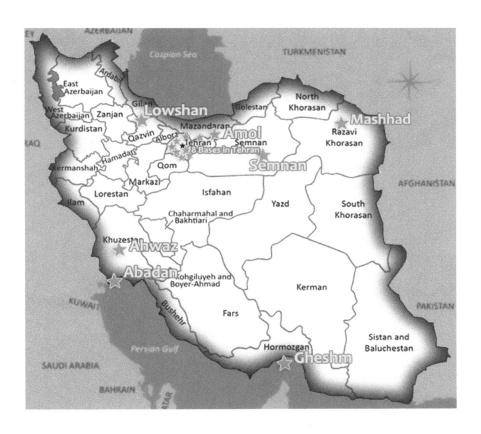

Location of 8 IRGC Terrorist Training Camps in Tehran

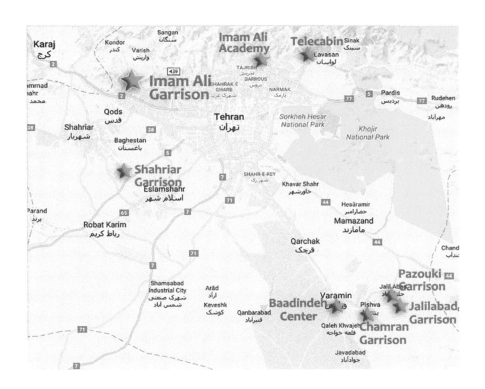

Imam Ali Garrison

IRGC's Main Terrorist Training Camp for Foreign Nationals

Imam Ali Garrison is the headquarters of the Qods Force training directorate, as well as one of its main training centers. This site is used for both short-term basic training, as well as full military training with specialized courses for those who are hired by the Quds Force on a permanent basis. Terrorist training courses are given as well in separate, secret units for dispatch to various countries in the Persian Gulf area, Asia, Africa, and Latin America.

Imam Ali Academy

IRGC's Theoretical Training Camp for Foreign Nationals

Located north of Saad Abad Palace, Alborz Street in Tajrish, Northern Tehran, IRGC mercenaries are first sent to this center for theoretical courses on fundamentalism and terrorism, and then sent to other centers for practical training. This site was previously used for practical terrorist training, but after it was exposed, practical military and terrorist training regimens were moved to the Imam Ali Garrison.

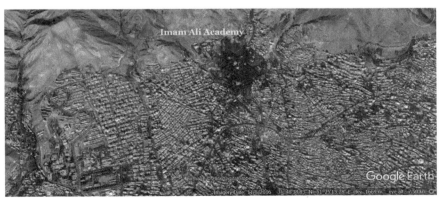

Lowshan Garrison

IRGC's Special Training Camp for Foreign Nationals

IRGC has a garrison near the city of Manjil, near the town of Lowshan; a portion of this garrison is provided to the Qods Force for training purposes.

Pazouki Garrison

IRGC's Training Camp for Afghan Nationals

In each session, 200 Afghans are trained at this garrison for deployment to Syria, where they are assigned to the Fatemiyoun Division. Infantry training includes Kalashnikovs, machine guns, mortars, tactics, sniper, and others. All instructors are from the Iranian Revolutionary Guards and the Quds Force.

Badindeh Garrison

IRGC's Urban Warfare and Terrorist Training Camp for Foreign Nationals

Urban warfare and terrorist training, including use of motorcycles for terrorist operations, is given. Driving courses and various vehicle-maneuvering courses are provided in this center. One of these exercises related to freeing hostages is carried out inside buildings designated for training.

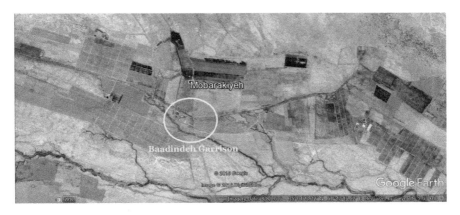

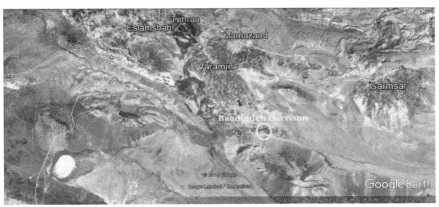

IRGC Command Chart

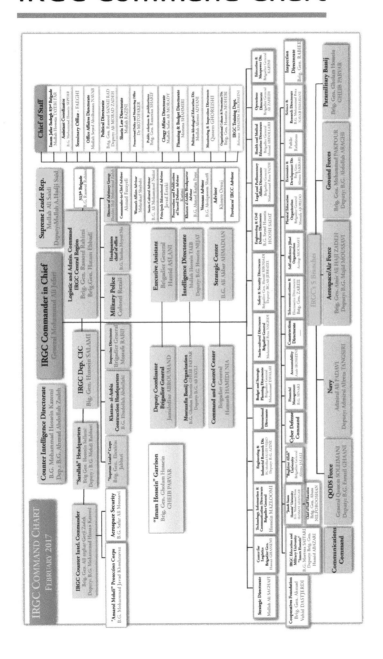

About NCRI-US

National Council of Resistance of Iran-US Representative Office acts as the Washington office for Iran's Parliament-in-exile, which is dedicated to the establishment of a democratic, secular, non-nuclear republic in Iran.

NCRI-US, registered as a non-profit tax-exempt organization, has been instrumental in exposing the nuclear weapons program of Iran, including the sites in Natanz, and Arak, the biological and chemical weapons program of Iran, as well as its ambitious ballistic missile program.

NCRI-US has also exposed the terrorist network of the Iranian regime, including its involvement in the bombing of Khobar Towers in Saudi Arabia, the Jewish Community Center in Argentina, its fueling of sectarian violence in Iraq and Syria, and its malign activities in other parts of the Middle East.

Our office has provided information on the human rights violations in Iran, extensive anti-government demonstrations, and the movement for democratic change in Iran.

Visit our website at **www.ncrius.org**

You may follow us on twitter @ncrius

Follow us on facebook. NCRIUS

You can also find us on Instagram NCRIUS

List of Publications

by the National Council of Resistance of Iran, U.S. Representative Office

Presidential Elections in Iran: Changing Faces; Status Quo Policies

May 2017, 78 pages

The book, reviews the past 11 presidential elections, demonstrating that the only criterion for qualifying as a candidate is practical and heartfelt allegiance to the Supreme Leader. An unelected vetting watchdog, the Guardian Council makes that determination.

The Rise of Iran's Revolutionary Guards' Financial Empire: How the Supreme Leader and the IRGC Rob the People to Fund International Terror

March 2017, 174 pages

This manuscript examines some vital factors and trends, including the overwhelming and accelerating influence (especially since 2005) of the Supreme Leader and the Islamic Revolutionary Guard Corps (IRGC). This study shows how ownership of property in various spheres of the economy is gradually shifted from the population writ large towards a minority ruling elite comprised of the Supreme Leader's office and the IRGC, using 14 powerhouses, and how the money ends up funding terrorism worldwide.

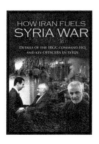

How Iran Fuels Syria War: Details of the IRGC Command HQ and Key Officers in Syria

November 2016, 74 pages

This book examines how the Iranian regime has effectively engaged in the military occupation of Syria by marshaling 70,000 forces, including the Islamic Revolutionary Guard Corps (IRGC) and mercenaries from other countries into Syria; is paying monthly salaries to over 250,000 militias and agents to prolong the conflict; divided the country into 5 zones of conflict and establishing 18 command, logistics and operations centers.

Nowruz 2016 with the Iranian Resistance: Hoping for a New Day, Freedom and Democracy in Iran

April 2016, 36 pages

This book describes Iranian New Year, Nowruz celebrations at the Washington office of Iran's parliament-in-exile, the National Council of Resistance of Iran. The yearly event marks the beginning of spring. It includes select speeches by dignitaries who have attended the NCRIUS Nowruz celebrations. This book also discusses the very rich culture and the traditions associated with Nowruz for centuries.

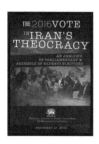

The 2016 Vote in Iran's Theocracy: An analysis of Parliamentary & Assembly of Experts Elections

February 2016, 70 pages

This book examines all the relevant data about the 2016 Assembly of Experts as well as Parliamentary elections ahead of the February 26, 2016 elections date. It looks at the history of such elections since the 1979 revolution and highlights the current intensified infighting among the various factions of the Iranian regime.

IRAN: A Writ of Deception and Cover-up: Iranian Regime's Secret Committee Hid Military Dimensions of its Nuclear Program

February 2016, 30 pages

The book provides details about a top-secret committee in charge of forging the answers to the International Atomic Energy Agency (IAEA) regarding the Possible Military Dimensions (PMD) of Tehran's nuclear program, including those related to the explosive detonators called EBW (Exploding Bridge Wire) detonator, which is an integral part of a program to develop an implosion type nuclear device.

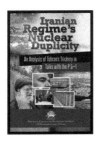

Iranian Regime's Nuclear Duplicity: An Analysis of Tehran's Trickery in Talks with the P 5+1

January 2016, 74 pages

This book examines Iran's behavior throughout the negotiations process in an effort to inform the current dialogue on a potential agreement. Drawing on both publicly available sources and those within Iran, the book focuses on two major periods of intense negotiations with the regime: 2003-2004 and 2013-2015. Based on this evidence, it then extracts the principles and motivations behind Tehran's approach to negotiations as well as the tactics used to trick its counterparts and reach its objectives.

Key to Countering Islamic Fundamentalism: Maryam Rajavi? Testimony To The U.S. House Foreign Affairs Committee

June 2015, 68 pages

Testimony before U.S. House Foreign Affairs Committee's subcommittee on Terrorism, non-Proliferation, and Trade discussing ISIS and Islamic fundamentalism. The book contains Maryam Rajavi's full testimony as well as the question and answer by representatives.

Meet the National Council of Resistance of Iran

June 2014, 150 pages

Meet the National Council of Resistance of Iran discusses what NCRI stands for, what its platform is, what it has done so far, and why a vision for a free, democratic, secular, non-nuclear republic in Iran would serve the world peace

How Iran Regime Cheated the World: Tehran's Systematic Efforts to Cover Up its Nuclear Weapons Program

June 2014, 50 pages

This book deals with one of the most fundamental challenges that goes to the heart of the dispute regarding the Iranian regime's controversial nuclear program: to ascertain with certainty that Tehran will not pursue a nuclear bomb. Such an assurance can only be obtained through specific steps taken by Tehran in response to the international community's concerns. The monograph discusses the Iranian regime's report card as far as it relates to being transparent when addressing the international community's concerns about the true nature and the ultimate purpose of its nuclear program

CPSIA information can be obtained
at www.ICGtesting.com
Printed in the USA
LVHW070851161219
640636LV00022B/498/P

9 781944 942069